Mosquitoes

by Sally M. Walker

Lerner Publications Company • Minneapolis

The photographs in this book are used with permission of: © Dwight R. Kuhn, pp. 4, 7, 11, 12, 13, 15, 19, 22, 27, 31, 34, 35, 48 (top); © David McNew/Getty Images, p. 5; Centers for Disease Control and Prevention Public Health Image Library/James Gathany, pp. 6, 10, 17, 20, 23, 25, 28, 37, 38, 46; © Scott Camazine/Photo Researchers, Inc., p. 8; © Joel Sartore/ National Geographic/Getty Images, p. 9; © Nature's Images/Photo Researchers, Inc., p. 14; © Michael Durham/Visuals Unlimited, p. 16; © Wim van Egmond/Visuals Unlimited, p. 18; © R.F. Ashley/Visuals Unlimited, p. 21; © Ken Preston-Mafham/PREMAPHOTOS/naturepl.com, p. 24; © Hans Pfletschinger/Peter Arnold, Inc., p. 26; © age fotostock/SuperStock, pp. 29, 33; © G.I. Bernard/Photo Researchers, Inc., p. 30; © Dr. Robert Calentine/Visuals Unlimited, p. 32; AP Photo/Ed Andrieski, p. 36; © Rick Poley/Visuals Unlimited, p. 39; Centers for Disease Control and Prevention Public Health Image Library, pp. 40, 41; AP Photo/The Daily Oakland Press, Doug Bauman, p. 42; AP Photo/Kevork Djansezian, p. 43; Agricultural Research Service, USDA, p. 47; © David McNew/Getty Images, p. 48 (bottom).

Front cover: Agricultural Research Service, USDA.

Lerner Publications Company
A division of Lerner Publishing Group, Inc.
241 First Avenue North
Minneapolis, MN 55401 U.S.A.

Website address: www.lernerbooks.com

Library of Congress Cataloging-in-Publication Data

Walker, Sally M.
    Mosquitoes / by Sally M. Walker.
       p. cm. — (Early bird nature books)
    Includes index.
    ISBN 978–0–8225–1375–9 (lib. bdg. : alk. paper)
    1. Mosquitoes—Juvenile literature. I. Title.
 QL536.W35 2009
 595.77'2—dc22   2007044318

Manufactured in the United States of America
1 2 3 4 5 6 – PA – 14 13 12 11 10 09

Contents

Be a Word Detective 5

Chapter 1 **The Mosquito**. 6

Chapter 2 **Body Parts** 10

Chapter 3 **An Itchy Bite** 19

Chapter 4 **Growing Up** 24

Chapter 5 **Mosquito Danger** 35

On Sharing a Book 44
A NOTE TO ADULTS

Learn More about Mosquitoes 45

Glossary. 46

Index 48

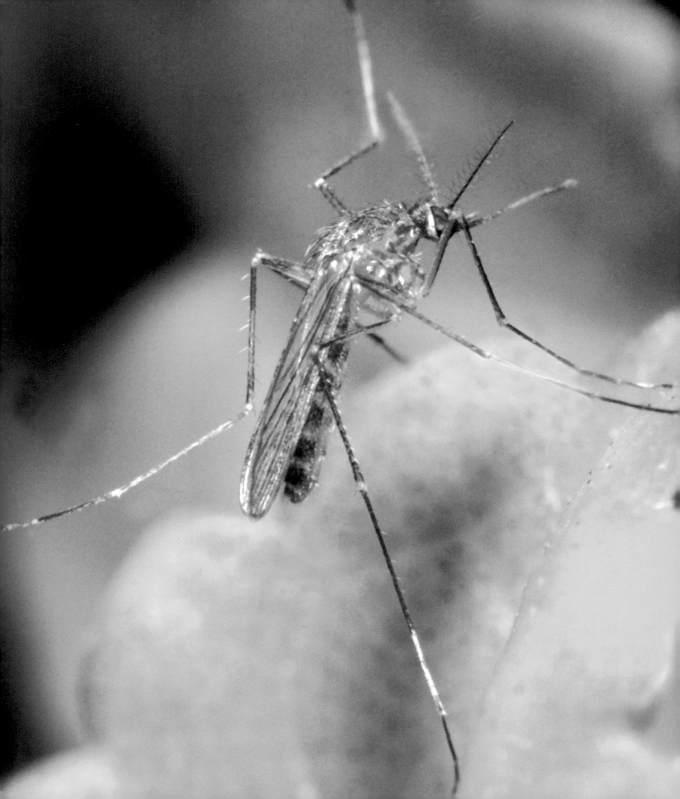

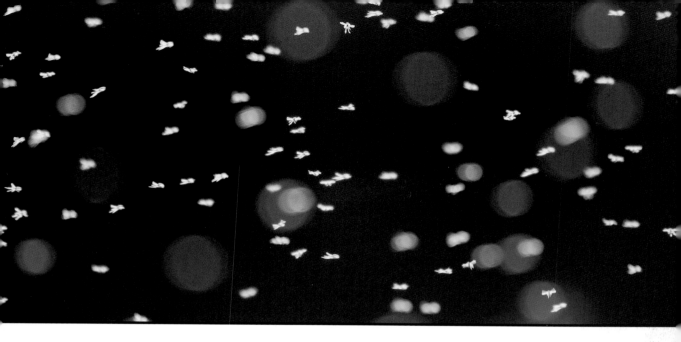

Be a Word Detective

Can you find these words as you read about mosquitoes?
Be a detective and try to figure out what they mean.
You can turn to the glossary on page 46 for help.

abdomen	**insects**	**proboscis**
antennas	**labium**	**pupa**
compound eyes	**larvas**	**siphon**
egg raft	**molting**	**stylets**
insecticides	**palpus**	**thorax**

There is more than one way to form plurals of some words.
The word antenna *has two possible plural endings—either*
an e *or an* s. *In this book,* s *is used when many antennas*
are being discussed.

Chapter 1

This mosquito is drinking blood from a person's hand. What kind of animal is a mosquito?

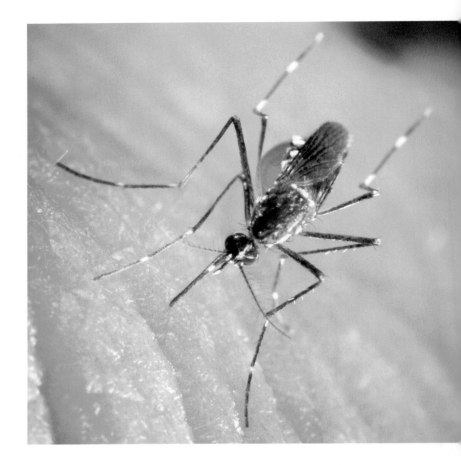

The Mosquito

It's summertime. You have just settled into bed. Suddenly, you hear a high-pitched hum. EEEEE. Oh no, it's a mosquito!

Mosquitoes are insects. Insects have hard skeletons on the outside of their bodies. Adult insects have six legs. Most insects have one or two pairs of wings. Mosquitoes have one pair.

A dragonfly (right) *tries to catch a mosquito. Dragonflies are insects with two pairs of wings.*

There are more than 2,500 species, or kinds, of mosquitoes. They live all over the world. Some mosquitoes live only in warm places. Cold weather kills them. Other mosquitoes live in cold places. The eggs of mosquitoes that live in the Arctic can withstand very cold winters. Common house mosquitoes live almost everywhere people do.

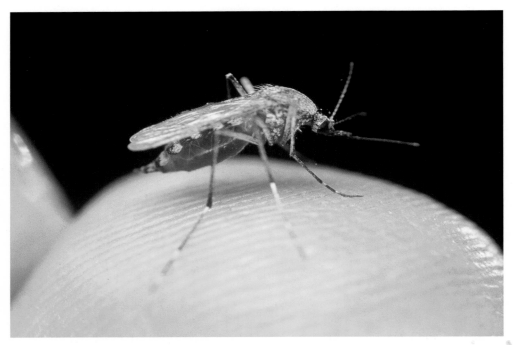

The scientific name of the common house mosquito is Culex pipiens.

These mosquitoes were resting in the grass in Alaska.
They came out of the grass to feed.

Mosquitoes rest among leaves and in the grass. They fly from their resting places to find food or a mate. Females fly to find places to lay their eggs.

Some species of mosquitoes are active in the early morning or in the evening. Some are active when it's sunny. Others are active at night or on cloudy days.

Chapter 2

Mosquitoes have three main body parts. Do you know what they are?

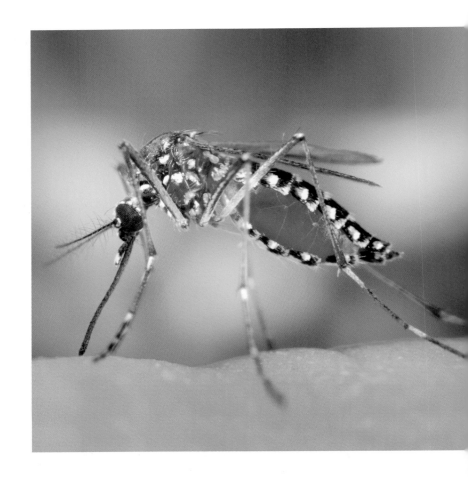

Body Parts

Like all insects, mosquitoes have three main body parts. They are the head, the thorax, and the abdomen (AB-duh-muhn).

A mosquito has two large eyes on its head. They are compound eyes. Compound eyes are made of many tiny lenses. A lens is the place where light enters the eyes. A mosquito's eyes do not see objects clearly. But they easily sense movements such as swatting hands or tails.

Mosquitoes have two compound eyes. Their tiny lenses look very colorful in this photo.

A mosquito has two antennas (an-TEH-nuhz) on its head. Each antenna has hairs on it. A male's antennas have very long, feathery hairs. A female has shorter and fewer hairs on her antennas.

Antennas are used to hear and smell. A male mosquito uses his antennas to listen for the hum of a female's wings.

A female mosquito uses her thin antennas to help her find a blood meal.

A mosquito's mouthparts are called a proboscis (pruh-BAHS-kuhs). A proboscis has several parts. Some are sharp and used for biting. Others carry liquid to or from the bite.

A mosquito has a palpus on each side of the proboscis. The palpi are used to touch and taste. Some mosquitoes have palpi that are as long as the proboscis.

This male mosquito has feathery antennas and long palpi. Its proboscis sticks out from between the palpi.

The thorax is the second main part of a mosquito's body. It is behind the head. A mosquito's six legs are attached to its thorax. Each leg has a foot with two claws. They help the mosquito cling to walls, plants, and animals.

This mosquito is clinging to a plant with the claws on its feet.

A mosquito folds back its two long wings when it isn't flying.

A pair of wings is also attached to the thorax. Each wing has thin lines called veins. Veins carry blood to the wings. They help stiffen the wings.

This male mosquito is flying at night.

A mosquito's wings often beat faster than 500 times per second. A flying mosquito can hover in one place or zigzag through the air. It can fly as fast as 3 miles per hour.

Beating wings make the humming sound that we hear. The wings of each species make their own special hum. Some hums are very high-pitched. Others are lower.

A mosquito's abdomen is behind its thorax. The abdomen contains the mosquito's stomach. A mosquito breathes through holes on the sides of its abdomen and thorax. Air flows into the holes. Tubes in the mosquito's body carry the air to the rest of its body.

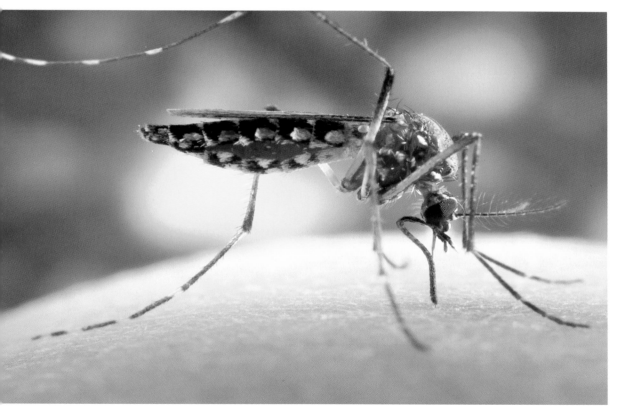

The stomach of this female mosquito is filling up with blood from her meal.

Tiny scales cover most parts of a mosquito. Scales help protect the body, legs, and wings. When the scales are touched, they rub off like powder. Scales can be many colors, including blue, white, green, and yellow.

When you look closely at a mosquito, you can see the scales that cover its body.

Chapter 3

Male mosquitoes don't suck blood. They suck the juice from fruits. What do females drink?

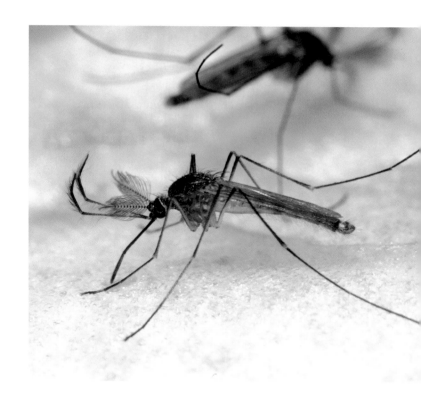

An Itchy Bite

Most mosquitoes suck nectar and juice from flowers and fruit. The females also suck blood. Some females bite certain animals, such as birds or frogs. But the females of other species suck blood from large animals or people.

A mosquito's proboscis has several cutting and sucking tools. They are covered by the labium. The labium is like a lip. Stylets are inside the labium. They are like needles. The stylets stab through the skin of an animal or person. The labium slides backward as the stylets dig deeper. The stylets stab the skin as many as 20 times in each bite. The mosquito does this to find the best place to suck blood.

This photograph shows the labium folded backward.

A thin tube in the proboscis pumps saliva into the bite. Saliva is the liquid animals have in their mouths. Chemicals in the saliva help thin the blood. They make the blood easier to suck. They also make a mosquito bite swell and itch.

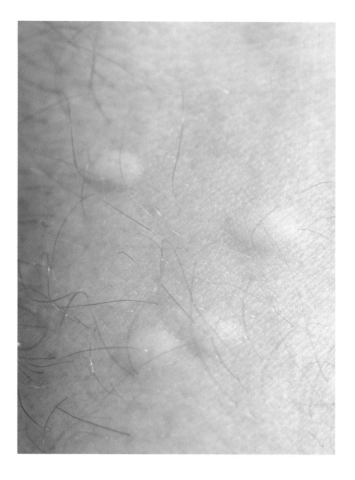

This man has four mosquito bites on his arm. Have you ever been bitten by a mosquito?

In 90 seconds, a female can suck enough blood to double or triple her body's weight. Her stomach stretches as blood flows into it. When her stomach is full, special signals are sent to the rest of her body. They tell her to stop sucking. Then she pulls out the stylets. The labium slides forward and covers the stylets again.

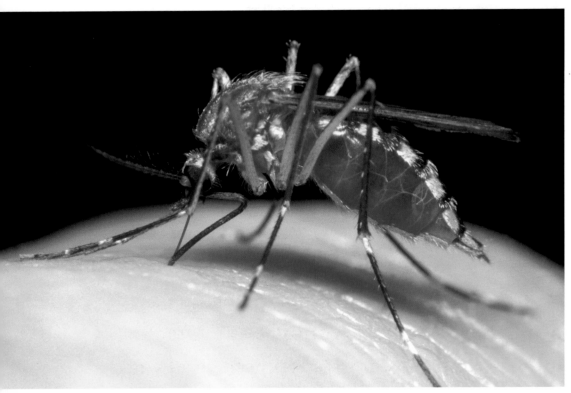

The stomach of a female mosquito gets bigger as she sucks blood.

This full mosquito has to work extra hard to fly away from her meal.

After a meal, the female is too heavy to fly far. She rests and takes in nutrients from the blood. Nutrients are things that help living things to grow. Water from the blood quickly passes through and out her body. After 45 minutes, the mosquito is ready to fly away. Nutrients from the blood will feed her eggs.

Chapter 4

This female mosquito is laying eggs on a pond. Where do other mosquitoes lay their eggs?

Growing Up

Mosquitoes lay their eggs in many different places. Some lay their eggs in water. One kind of mosquito lays its eggs only in water found on the leaves of the pitcher plant. Others lay eggs in places that will get wet in the future. These mosquitoes often pick holes in trees or the ground.

Some species lay their eggs separately. The eggs look like boats called canoes. Each side of the egg has a float on it. The floats keep the egg from tipping upside down.

One egg from an Aedes aegypti *mosquito floats on the water.*

Other species lay their eggs in egg rafts.
To do this, the female stands on the water.
She squeezes an egg out a hole in the tip of
her abdomen. The egg looks like a tiny grain
of dark brown rice. One end is more pointed
than the other end.

*This female mosquito is making an egg raft
with her eggs.*

The female lays more eggs. Each new egg is placed next to the one laid before it. She stands each egg on its end, with the pointed tip upward. Her legs help hold the eggs in place. The female lays several rows of eggs. The packed rows of eggs form a raft. The outer edges of the raft are higher than the middle part. This stops the raft from tipping over.

The eggs that make up this egg raft are packed tightly together.

Baby mosquitoes that hatch from eggs are called larvas. Larvas need water to hatch. Some larvas hatch within a few days. Larvas in eggs laid in dry or cool places may not hatch for months or even years. In certain deserts, larvas must wait 10 or more years for the water they need to hatch.

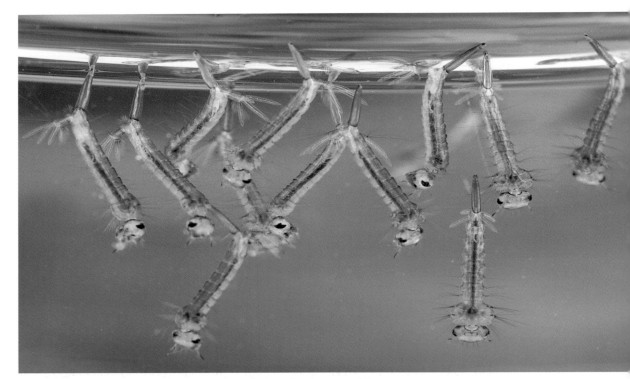

Mosquito larvas hatch in water. They hang upside down and eat.

These larvas are breathing through tubes that stick out of the water.

All larvas live in water. Some larvas breathe through a tube called a siphon (SY-fuhn). The siphon is on the larva's abdomen. It sticks out of the water.

One kind of larva sinks. It gets air from the roots of plants. First, the larva scrapes a hole in a cattail root. Then it sticks its siphon into the hole. The larva sucks in air from the cattail's root.

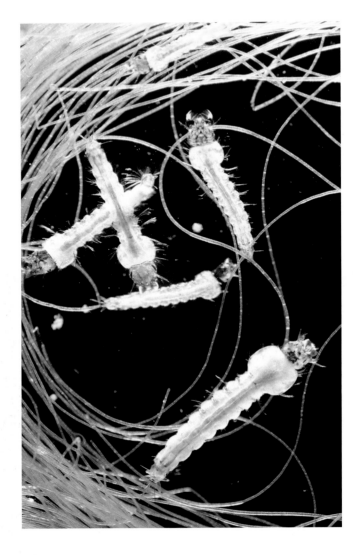

The larvas of Anopheles mosquitoes float below the surface of the water.

Some larvas don't have siphons. Long hairs on their bodies keep them floating on the surface. They breathe through holes in their abdomens.

A larva spends most of its time eating tiny creatures. Soon the larva grows too big for its skin. The larva sheds its tight skin. Shedding an old skin is called molting. The larva wriggles out of its old skin. New skin already covers its body.

This mosquito larva has just molted. It is eating its old skin to get the nutrients to keep growing.

In four to ten days, the larva will molt four times. After the fourth molt, it is called a pupa (PYOO-puh). The pupa is shaped like a giant comma. Flat paddles on the end of the abdomen help the pupa swim. Thin skin covers the parts that will become its body, wings, and legs.

Mosquito pupas are also called tumblers. When a pupa swims, it looks as if it is tumbling through the water.

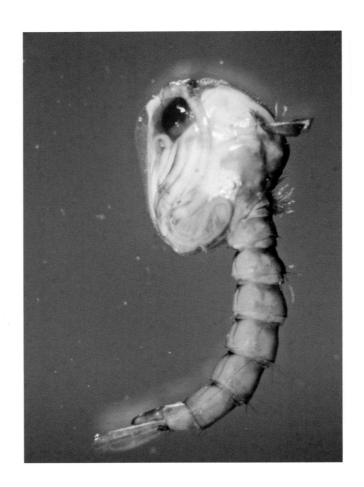

A pupa takes in air through two breathing tubes. They look like trumpets that poke above the water's surface. A pupa does not eat. All of its energy goes into growing.

Like larvas, pupas live and grow underwater. They breathe the air that is above the water. Can you see these pupas' breathing tubes?

In two to four days, the pupa's skin splits open. An adult mosquito climbs out. It floats on the shed skin until its wings dry. After 30 minutes, the adult is ready to fly away.

Male mosquitoes only live a few days or weeks. Females live longer than males. Some live as long as five to six months.

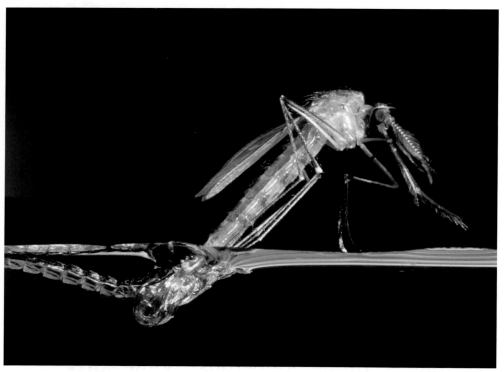

This adult mosquito is coming out of its pupa stage. Soon it will fly away.

Chapter 5

This is an Asian tiger mosquito. It can be very dangerous to humans. Do you know why?

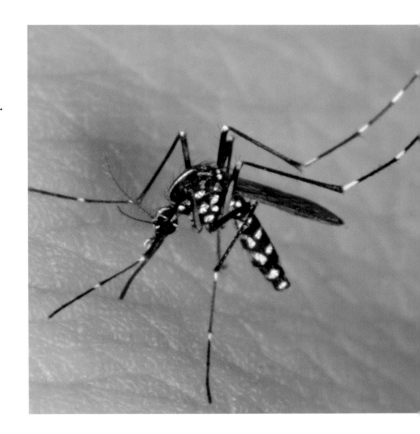

Mosquito Danger

Mosquitoes play an important role in nature. Many animals eat them. But mosquitoes can be dangerous. Some carry germs that cause sickness.

Mosquitoes can spread yellow fever, West Nile virus, and dengue (DEHN-gee) fever. These diseases are caused by viruses. Viruses are living things that can only be seen under a microscope. Viruses live inside the bodies of larger living things.

This woman survived the West Nile virus. Female mosquitoes can pick up the virus when they feed on the blood of birds that have it.

Mosquitoes also spread malaria. Malaria is caused by a parasite. A parasite is a creature that feeds and lives on another living creature.

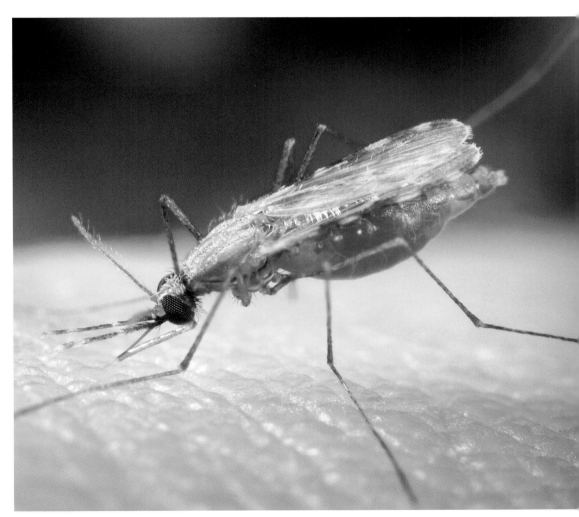

This species of Anopheles *mosquito can carry malaria parasites from person to person. Malaria kills about one million people each year.*

The Aedes aegypti *mosquito can pass the dengue fever virus to humans when she feeds on their blood.*

A virus or parasite may be in the blood that a female mosquito sucks. The virus or parasite spreads inside the mosquito's body and saliva. But it doesn't harm the mosquito. When the mosquito bites a person, its saliva carries the virus or parasite into the person's body. Then the person may become sick.

It is important to protect people from diseases carried by mosquitoes. One way is by killing mosquitoes with insecticides (ihn-SEHK-tuh-syds). Insecticides are chemicals that kill insects. But insecticides can be dangerous too. They may harm plants and other animals.

This airplane is spraying an insecticide to kill mosquitoes and prevent the spread of the diseases that they carry.

Another way to protect people from mosquitoes is to clean up wet places where mosquitoes lay their eggs. The water may be inside old tires, cans, or even a toy. When people empty the water from these containers, mosquitoes have fewer places to lay eggs.

Rain can fill old tires like these with water. Female mosquitoes may lay their eggs in the water.

Some mosquito larvas can help kill mosquitoes too. Toxorhynchites are a kind of mosquito that never suck blood. Their larvas eat only the larvas of other mosquitoes. Then there are fewer blood-sucking mosquitoes to spread disease.

People in some places are using mosquito fish to control mosquitoes. These small fish eat mosquito larvas.

A mosquito fish is about to eat a mosquito larva.

These students are putting up bat houses. Bats eat mosquitoes.

Hanging houses in your yard for bats and birds will help control the number of mosquitoes around your house. Why? Because bats and birds gobble up hundreds of mosquitoes a day!

Almost anywhere people go, they are sure to find mosquitoes. We must keep learning about them. The more we know, the better able we will be to live with mosquitoes of all kinds.

This father is spraying mosquito repellent on his son. Repellents help keep mosquitoes from biting.

ON SHARING A BOOK

When you share a book with a child, you show that reading is important. To get the most out of the experience, read in a comfortable, quiet place. Turn off the television and limit other distractions, such as telephone calls.

Be prepared to start slowly. Take turns reading parts of this book. Stop occasionally and discuss what you're reading. Talk about the photographs. If the child begins to lose interest, stop reading. When you pick up the book again, revisit the parts you have already read.

BE A VOCABULARY DETECTIVE

The word list on page 5 contains words that are important in understanding the topic of this book. Be word detectives and search for the words as you read the book together. Talk about what the words mean and how they are used in the sentence. Do any of these words have more than one meaning? You will find the words defined in a glossary on page 46.

WHAT ABOUT QUESTIONS?

Use questions to make sure the child understands the information in this book. Here are some suggestions:

> What did this paragraph tell us? What does this picture show? What do you think we'll learn about next? Where do mosquitoes live? How do mosquitoes feed? What are young mosquitoes called after they hatch from eggs? What is your favorite part of this book? Why?

If the child has questions, don't hesitate to respond with questions of your own, such as What do *you* think? Why? What is it that you don't know? If the child can't remember certain facts, turn to the index.

INTRODUCING THE INDEX

The index helps readers find information without searching through the whole book. Turn to the index on page 48. Choose an entry such as *legs* and ask the child to find out how many legs mosquitoes have. Repeat with as many entries as you like. Ask the child to point out the differences between an index and a glossary. (The index helps readers find information, while the glossary tells readers what words mean.)

LEARN MORE ABOUT
MOSQUITOES

BOOKS

Fredericks, Anthony D. *Bloodsucking Creatures.* New York: Franklin Watts, 2002. Learn about mosquitoes, lampreys, leeches, ticks, lice, mites, vampire bats, and other creatures that feed on blood.

Sill, Cathryn. *About Insects: A Guide for Children.* Atlanta: Peachtree, 2000. This beautifully illustrated book explains the basic characteristics, behaviors, and habitats of various insects.

Siy, Alexandra, and Dennis Kunkel. *Mosquito Bite.* Watertown, MA: Charlesbridge, 2005. Learn more about the mosquito's life cycle in exciting microscopic detail.

WEBSITES

Hey! A Mosquito Bit Me!
http://www.kidshealth.org/kid/ill_injure/bugs/mosquito.html
This KidsHealth page describes what to do if a mosquito bites and how to avoid getting bitten.

Mosquito
http://www.enchantedlearning.com/subjects/insects/mosquito/
Mosquito
Print out diagrams of a mosquito's body and life cycle on this site from Enchanted Learning.

GLOSSARY

abdomen (AB-duh-muhn): the back part of a mosquito's body

antennas (an-TEH-nuhz): long, thin feelers on a mosquito's head that allow it to hear and smell

compound eyes: eyes made up of many small lenses

egg raft: a group of mosquito eggs that stick together and float in water. They look like a raft.

insecticides (ihn-SEHK-tuh-syds): chemicals used to kill insects

insects: animals with six legs and three main body parts. Most insects have wings.

labium: the lower lip of a mosquito

larvas: young mosquitoes that have hatched from their eggs

molting: shedding old skin to make way for new, larger skin

palpus: a body part next to a mosquito's mouthparts that it uses to touch and taste

proboscis (pruh-BAHS-kuhs): the long, hollow part of a mosquito that it uses to suck blood or plant juices

pupa (PYOO-puh): a young mosquito covered in a thin skin. A mosquito becomes a pupa after it is a larva and before it is an adult.

siphon (SY-fuhn): a tubelike body part that a larva uses to breathe

stylets: mouthparts that a mosquito uses for cutting

thorax: the middle part of a mosquito's body

INDEX

Pages listed in **bold** type refer to photographs.

antennas, 12, **13**

babies, 28–33, 41
body, 7, 10–18, 22, 31, 32
breathing, 17, 29–30, 33

dangers to mosquitoes, 35,
   39–42
diseases from mosquitoes,
   36–39

eggs, 8, 9, 23, 24–28, 40
eyes, 11

feeding, 6, 9, 13, **17**, 20–22, 28,
   31, **36**, 38
flying, 9, 16, 23, 34
food, **6**, 9, **12**, 19, 23, 31

hair, 12, 30
head, 10–13
homes, 8–9, 24, 29, **33**

kinds of mosquitoes, 8, 24–25,
   26, 29–30, 41

legs, 7, 14, 18, 27, 32

mouthparts, 13, 20

people and mosquitoes, 35–43

sounds, 6, 12, 16

wings, 7, 15–16, 18, 32, 34